All of these words appear in the book.
Try to match the word and picture stickers.

galaxy   observatory   Yuri Gagarin   crater

Mercury   Venus   Earth   Mars   Jupiter   Sun

Uranus   Neptune   comet   asteroid   Saturn

Eris   satellite   Laika   satellite dish   shuttle

astronaut   probe   Voyager

International Space Station   Isaac Newton

Galileo Galilei   Stephen Hawking   meteor

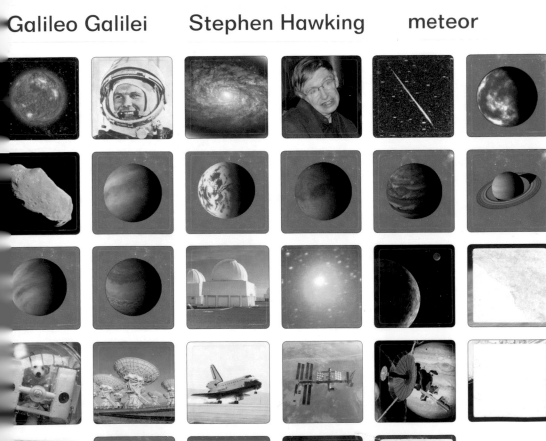

Space

Written by Janine Amos
Reading consultants: Christopher Collier and Alan Howe,
Bath Spa University, UK

This edition published by Parragon in 2011
Parragon
Queen Street House
4 Queen Street
Bath BA1 1HE, UK

ISBN 978-1-4075-1833-6

Printed in China

space

PaRragon

Bath • New York • Singapore • Hong Kong • Cologne • Delhi
Melbourne • Amsterdam • Johannesburg • Auckland • Shenzhen

Parents' notes

This book is part of a series of non-fiction books designed to appeal to children learning to read.

Each book has been developed with the help of educational experts.

At the end of each book is a quiz to help your child remember the information and the meanings of some of the words and sentences. There is also a glossary of difficult words relating to the subject matter in the book, and an index.

Contents

Night sky

When you look at the night sky you can see thousands of stars. They are so far away that they look tiny. But really they are giant balls of glowing gas.

Our Sun is a star.

All the stars we can see are part of our galaxy. A galaxy is a massive group of stars.

The temperature at the heart of a star reaches over 16 million degrees celsius.

The universe is made up of everything in time and space. It is growing all the time.

There are a lot of galaxies in the universe. Our galaxy is called the Milky Way.

Our star

Our star is called the Sun. The Earth and the other planets travel around the Sun.

The Sun is our closest star. It is more than a million times bigger than the Earth.

Amazing!

The centre of the Sun is like a massive bomb — it is always exploding!

The planets travel around the Sun along a path called an orbit. As they go, they spin around and around like tops. They are kept in their orbit by a force called gravity.

The Earth orbits the Sun. It takes about 365 days, or one year.

The Moon orbits the Earth. This takes about one month.

The planets

All the planets that orbit the Sun are different. On some the air is poisonous. Others are burning hot or freezing cold or covered in dust.

Mercury   Venus   Earth   Mars   Jupiter

The planets closest to the Sun are called inner planets. They are made mainly of rock and metal. The Earth is one of them.

The planets farthest from the Sun are called outer planets. They are huge balls made mainly of gas.

Saturn

Uranus

Neptune

Other space objects

Have you ever seen a shooting star streaking across the night sky? Space is not completely empty. There are dust, gas, rock and ice whizzing about at high speed.

Asteroids are massive space rocks. Most move around the Sun in a band called the asteroid belt.

This picture shows a huge crater in the USA. It was made by a meteor crashing into the Earth.

Every year, thousands of pieces of space rock fall onto the Earth. Most fall into the sea.

Comets are balls of ice with long, shining tails of dust and gas.

Meteors are made of burning space dust. We know them as 'shooting stars'.

Our solar system

The planets and their moons are part of our solar system. So is everything else that travels around the Sun, from the largest asteroid to the smallest speck of dust.

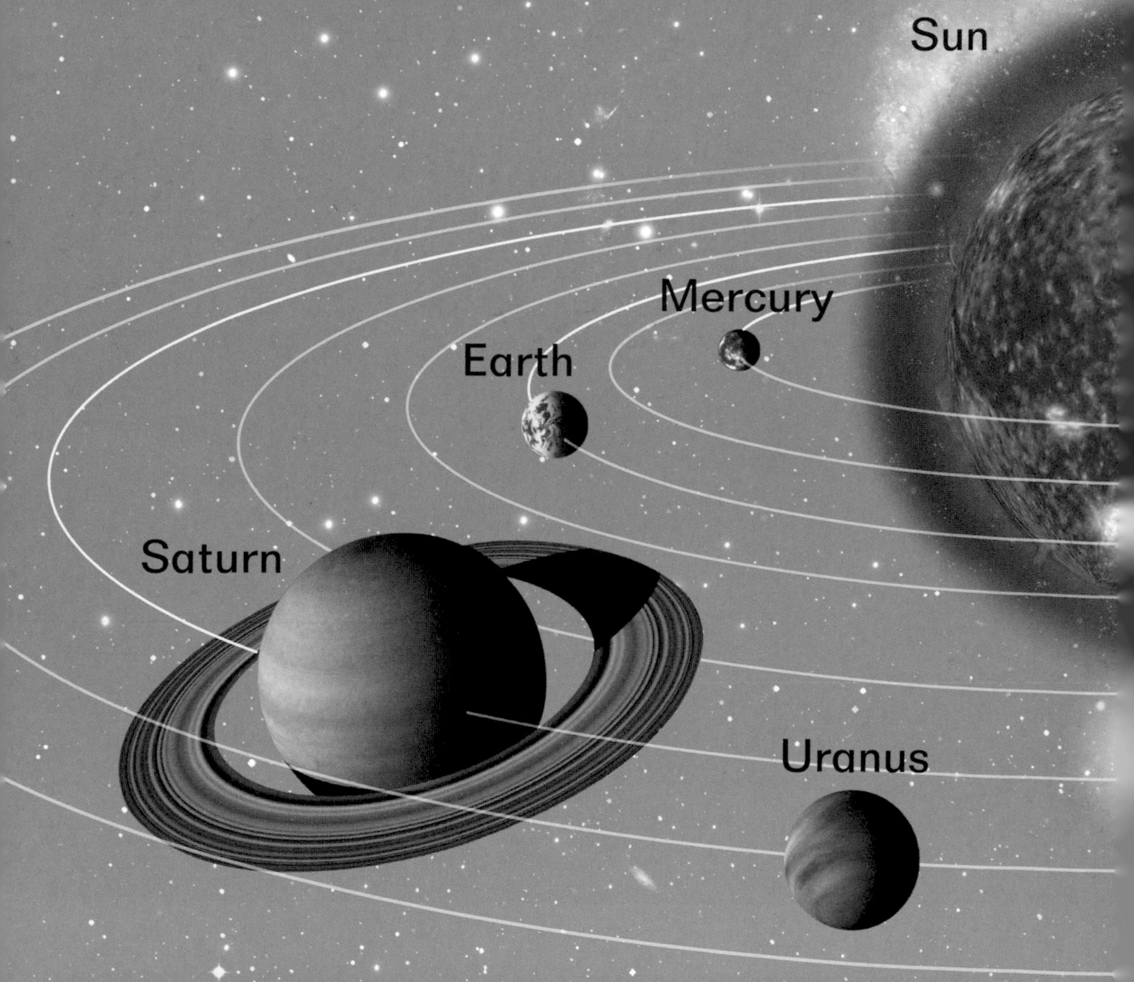

Sun

Mercury

Earth

Saturn

Uranus

Our solar system also contains at least four dwarf planets. Eris is the biggest dwarf planet.

Mars

Venus

Jupiter

Neptune

Looking into space

For hundreds of years people have used telescopes to look into space. Telescopes make far away objects look closer.

Big telescopes are kept in buildings called observatories. Most observatories are built on high land away from city lights.

A satellite dish collects radio waves given off by objects in space. In New Mexico, 27 dishes work together.

The Earth's atmosphere stops us from seeing some stars and planets. The Hubble Space Telescope orbits beyond the atmosphere so it can see more clearly into space.

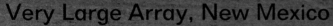

Very Large Array, New Mexico

Famous astronomers

People have been studying the universe for thousands of years. People who study space are called astronomers.

Galileo Galilei (1564–1642) was one of the first people to use a telescope to study the sky. He learned that the planets move around the Sun.

Stephen Hawking is studying the sky today. He believes that humans must find new homes on other planets.

Isaac Newton (1643–1727) worked out why the planets move around the Sun. He learned that a force called gravity keeps them circling there.

IOANNIS KEPPLERI
Mathematici Cæsarei
hanc Imaginem.
ARGENTORATENSI BIBLIOTHECÆ.
Confect.

Johannes Kepler (1571–1630) used mathematics to work out how the planets move.

William Herschel (1738–1822) built a huge telescope. His sister was also an astronomer.

Astronauts in space

Hundreds of people have travelled into space. Maybe one day you might travel into space, too.

Yuri Gagarin was the first person in space. He was a Russian cosmonaut. He travelled once around the Earth.

There is no air in space for sound to travel through. You can shout as loud as you like — and no one will hear you.

Neil Armstrong, an American astronaut, was the first person to walk on the Moon. His footprint is still there. There is no rain and no wind to blow it away.

Today, the Space Shuttle is launched by booster rockets. In less than 10 minutes, it reaches space.

Space station

A space station is a huge workplace in space. People carry out experiments there and collect information about the stars and planets.

The International Space Station

When astronauts work outside, they wear a special suit to protect them. They carry a backpack with air to breathe.

Crew members attach their sleeping bags to the station's walls for a good night's sleep.

There is microgravity in space. It makes you feel as if you are floating.

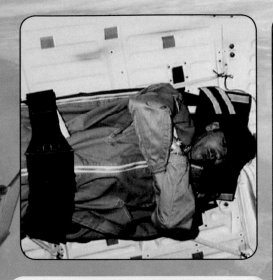

Amazing!

Which way is up? Astronauts attach themselves to their workstations with Velcro.

Objects will float about, too. Everything is strapped down – even meal trays.

Space probes

Robot probes explore places people cannot reach, and send information back to Earth.

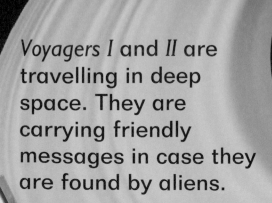

Voyagers I and *II* are travelling in deep space. They are carrying friendly messages in case they are found by aliens.

Two-thirds of probes sent to Mars have not completed their missions. It's called the Mars Curse!

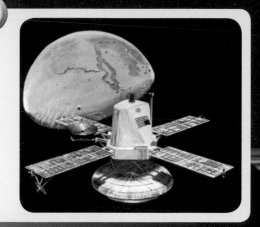

The probe *Galileo* travelled around Jupiter 34 times. It sent pictures and information back to the Earth.

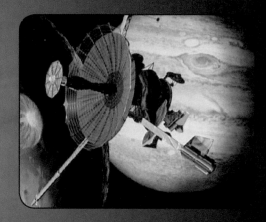

The *Cassini-Huygens* spacecraft reached Saturn and its moons in 2004. The Huygens probe can collect far more information than a human space explorer.

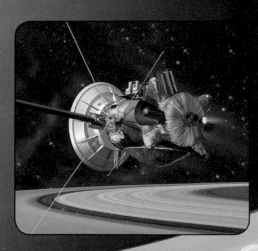

Quiz

Now try this quiz!
All the answers can be found in this book.

What is the name of our galaxy?

(a) The Doughnut
(b) The Chocolate Cake
(c) The Milky Way

Which was the first animal to be sent into space?

(a) A dog
(b) A cat
(c) A horse

Where do you put your sleeping bag in a space station?

(a) In a tent
(b) On the floor
(c) On the wall

How many days does it take the Earth to orbit the Sun?

(a) About 3 days
(b) About 36 days
(c) About 365 days

What is a comet made of?

(a) Ice
(b) Wood
(c) Potatoes

Who was the first person to travel into space?

(a) Neil Armstrong
(b) Yuri Gagarin
(c) Galileo Galilei

Glossary

Astronaut A person who is trained to travel in space.

Atmosphere The invisible cloak of air that surrounds the Earth. It is made up of gas, water and dust.

Cosmonaut A Russian astronaut.

Galaxy A large group of billions of stars.

Gravity The force that holds us to the ground and keeps the Earth in orbit around the Sun.

Microgravity A state of low gravity, where astronauts and objects in a space station appear to float.

Planet A large ball of rock or gas that travels around a star.

Probe   A spacecraft with no
                     crew that explores in
                     space and sends
                     information back
                     to the Earth.

Satellite   An object that travels
                     around a planet. A
                     natural satellite is also
                     called a moon. An
                     artificial satellite has
                     been made by humans.

Solar system   The group of planets,
                     comets and asteroids
                     that move around
                     the Sun.

Space   Everything beyond the
                     Earth's atmosphere.

Index

Acknowledgements

t=top, c=centre, b=bottom, r=right, l=left

Cover: NASA/Roger Ressmeyer/Corbis

p 5tl Reuters/Corbis, p 6cl Denis Scott/Corbis, p 6-7 Alessandro Della Bella/epa/Corbis, p 8-9 Denis Scott/Corbis, p 9tr Farhad Parsa/zefa/Corbis, p 9br Denis Scott/Corbis, p 10 Tim Kiusalaas/Corbis , p 11 Tim Kiusalaas/Corbis, p 12-13 Bryan Allen/Corbis, p 12cr NASA/JPL, p 13tr Denis Scott/CorbisJames, p 13cl Roger Ressmeyer/Corbis, p 13cr Reuters/Corbis, p 14-15 Denis Scott/Corbis, p 14 -15 Tim Kiusalaas/Corbis, p 16-17 Mark Chivers/Robert Harding World Imagery/Corbis, p 17tl NASA, p 17b Richard T. Nowitz/Corbis, p 16br Marc Garanger/Corbis, p 18l Bettmann/Corbis, p 19tr The Gallery Collection/Corbis, p 19cl Rune Hellestad/Corbis, p 19bl Bettmann/Corbis, p 19br Bettmann/Corbis, p 20-21 Corbis, p 20l Bettmann/Corbis, p 20r Stocktrek/Corbis, p 21bl Nasa, p 22c NASA via CNP, p 23tl NASA, p 23tr NASA, p 23bl nasa, p 23 br NASA, p 24-25 Time & Life Pictures/Getty Image, p 25tr NASA, p 25cr NASA/JSC, p 25br epa/Corbis, p 27c NASA/JPL, p 27b Denis Scott/Corbis, p 28-31 Bryan Allen/Corbis